How to Price Your Art
Pricing with Confidence
for Sales & Profit

by Matt Tommey

How to Price Your Art
Pricing with Confidence for Sales & Profit

Copyright © 2021 Matt Tommey. All rights reserved.
www.MattTommeyMentoring.com

This book or parts thereof may not be reproduced in any form, stored in a retrieval system, or transmitted in any form by any means—electronic, mechanical, photocopy, recording, or otherwise—without prior written permission of the author, except as provided by United States copyright law.

Table of Contents

Introduction 1
PART ONE: The Importance, Benefits and Motivation for Generating Profit 7
    Why Profit is Important 9
    Fulfilled Entrepreneur or Servant to Your Business 17
    Pricing Barriers 23
PART TWO: The Nitty Gritty of Pricing Your Work 29
    How to Make a Profit on Every Sale 31
    Additional Markup and Retail Pricing 37
    Additional Considerations When Pricing Your Work 43
PART THREE: Seven Factors that Affect Pricing 51
    Quality of the Work and Perception 53
    Reputation 57
    Ways to Enhance the Perception of Your Work .. 63
    Scarcity and Leverage 69
    Create a Client Niche 77

Frequently Asked Questions.................................83
Final Thoughts...89
For Further Reading..91
About the Author...93
Other Resources from Matt Tommey...................95

Introduction

Nobody becomes an artist just to worry about paying the bills. Or just to keep busy or to have a job. We become artists because we're not happy unless we're doing the thing we were created for. Because there is a burning inside that won't quit until we give it expression. We become artists because we can't do anything else and be authentic.

But many artists have a misconception about making money with their art. It is not delusional to believe you can be an artist that is both successful in selling your art *and* artistically creative and fulfilled.

An artist who makes a living from their creativity, is both an artist and an entrepreneur; and you have to think like both to be successful. In fact, approached in a balanced way, the roles of artist and entrepreneur actually fuel each other. Otherwise, you get to play the part of the starving artist. I believe you can be both extremely creative *and* true to your artistic passions while making a good living doing it. However, until an artist learns how to price their work with confidence, for sales and profit, this dream can easily elude them. I know because that was my story.

When I initially started selling my basketry work, I did what most artists do. I asked myself "What do I think this is worth" and "What do I think my friends or family would pay for this?" I also tried to predict what others would pay for my work by guessing what I considered affordable versus expensive. As a hobbyist just having fun with my baskets on the side, it wasn't that big of a deal. However, as I started becoming more serious about selling my work and trying to make a living from it – both part time and full time – my pricing strategy had to change!

As my business and art matured, I realized my most profitable sales were my most expensive unique pieces. In fact, it was easy to raise the prices on that line of work because price wasn't the leading factor for those clients. Connection with me and the work I created, as well as the aesthetic and uniqueness of my designs were the driving factors. Over time, a beautiful thing started to happen. I was making work I absolutely loved for prices that kept increasing, giving me more time to create, connect with clients and be inspired.

Unless you are making a profit with your art sales, you simply have a hobby. Hobbies are great, but they rarely get beyond being self-sustaining without a strategy for growth. If having a hobby is all you're looking for from your art, great! Enjoy! But for most artists, that's not the case (especially if you're reading this book!). And as I like to remind my students, you can't have business dreams with hobby habits.

And, if you're not pricing your artwork in a way that generates profit, you will end up frustrated. Why? Because you're spending time, energy and money on creating work that you're not being financially rewarded for. That often results in tons of unsold work sitting in the garage, feelings of inadequacy and a general frustration that you're not getting what you deserve from your work. This frustration is not only annoying, it's detrimental to your success because it creates a self-defeating mindset and takes your focus off of creating your best work. So how do you start to remedy this dilemma? Profit.

Thankfully, after many years, I discovered a methodology that has enabled me to price my work with confidence. Instead of using my best guess in pricing my art, the simple concepts I'm going to teach you here in this book paved the way for my business success. Without understanding how to price with profit in mind, I'd still be making baskets in the garage for fun on the weekends. Instead, I've been able to build a six-figure art business while thriving creatively and financially. And when you employ these concepts in your business, you'll have incredible results too!

PART ONE:
The Importance, Benefits and Motivation for Generating Profit

Why Profit is Important

It's vital we establish the importance and benefits of profit before we get into the nitty gritty of pricing our work.

Profit is commonly defined as the money that's left over after all your expenses have been paid. Usually, profits go to the owner of the business and/or can be reinvested back into the business to enable growth.

Profit Fuels Growth

Healthy growth happens in a business when the business owner has the time, energy and money to reinvest in their business. It's getting that larger studio space, new piece of equipment or a better website. It can even look like the ability to apply for better shows, investing in marketing materials, creating reproductions of your work or hiring a coach to help get you to the next level.

One of the greatest growth strategies I've employed in my art business was hiring a studio assistant. Hiring just one part-time person to create parts of my work that were production oriented while at the same time greeting customers in my studio and gallery had an exponential multiplying effect on my profits. What used to take me 2 weeks by myself now took only 3 days. This increased both my production and sales. It was the difference between making enough to get by to having more than enough with plenty left over. That's huge!

As you consider how you might use profit to fuel your business growth, consider these questions:

- What are the areas of your business that you'd like to grow?
- How would that affect your business productivity and profit?

- What equipment, studio space and team members do you need for the next phase of your business growth?

Guaranteed profit is the fuel to get you there.

Profit Buys Time for Creating

If you ask most artists what they want, the answer is often "more time creating in the studio." In fact, the subject of sales, business and profits can often make many artists cringe because it seems so disingenuous to the creative process. However, the opposite is true. The more you learn to connect with clients in the market and sell your work at prices that generate generous profits, the more time you will have to create the work you love. Pricing your art at rock-bottom discounted prices only hurts one person: you.

I remember when I began to focus more seriously on my woven sculpture work. I found a great studio in Asheville North Carolina's River Arts District and started doing some local shows in the area. I even garnered some accolades for my work. However, I was still using that old "what do I think this is worth" model of pricing and it was getting me nowhere. Not only was I not making significant money from my hard work and creative energy, I was creating a story around my work that wasn't helping me sell to my ideal clients. (We'll talk more about how pricing and perception work together later in Chapter 7.)

As I began to look for strategies to price my work more reasonably, I took inspiration from models my friends were using; primarily potters. They did a ton of wholesale work and consequently developed a pricing model based on volume. That works great if you can crank out multiple pieces a day, driving the price per piece down. Not so much if you're creating one of a kind sculptural works that can take days, if not weeks to create. I didn't want to spend hours creating work to sell at a low price point I wasn't passionate about just to make ends meet. I had my studio rent and expenses, not to mention paying myself. After a couple years working like this, I had to find a new approach that worked for me and the art I was creating. Pricing for profit can bring creative freedom into your life.

Profit Gives You Options

When you create work you love and find that connection point in the marketplace where you're selling at a profit on a regular basis, options begin to emerge. Yet many artists get trapped into making work that sells, rather than making work they are passionate about. Obviously, to make money and profit as an artist, your work has to sell, but that should never be at the expense of the creative process. Without genuine desire, ongoing inspiration and creative fulfillment, creating art simply becomes a production line, no different than creating cars on an assembly line.

The first option profit gives you is the option to make the work you love. The more money you make (and keep) the more room you have in your schedule to create, experiment and play during your creative process. That's invaluable when it comes to thriving as an artist.

As you consider your options, ask yourself these questions:

- How do you want to live your life?
- What's important to you?
- What does your ideal schedule look like?
- How much time do you want to spend making and running your art business versus enjoying your family and having fun?

Fulfilled Entrepreneur or Servant to Your Business

As we saw in the last chapter; profit allows you to intentionally craft your business in ways that bring you life and fulfillment. Instead of feeling inextricably tied to your business without margin to enjoy life, you can intentionally create a business that serves you. It also allows you to fully enjoy your life!

No artist has the luxury of living in a creative bubble, creating 24/7 with no other concerns or responsibilities. We are husbands and fathers, wives and mothers, sisters and brothers. We have mortgages, rent and car payments. We go to church, enjoy our friends, like to go on vacation and out to eat in nice restaurants. Just like everyone else, we have a life and profit enables us to enjoy it without the stress of barely making ends meet.

Unfortunately, most artists serve their business rather than creating an art business that serves them. What do I mean? Let me draw a clear comparison with just a few illustrations.

Serving My Business
Working all the time
Can't take time off because everything depends on you
Does every job all the time, resulting in lower productivity and frustration
Creating work that sells at price points that produce just enough to get by

My Business Serves Me
Working based on a reasonable schedule that fits your desired lifestyle
Enjoy regular vacations & time off in order to rest, relax and recharge
Employs a team to help manage the business (studio assistant, web designer, bookkeeper, etc.)
Creating work you love that attracts your ideal clients and sells for a profit

A thriving artist creates work they love with skill and excellence, always endeavoring to grow and improve artistically; all while they market and sell their work for top dollar. That's what I created in my business. It's also what I'm passionate about helping other artists do as well in their businesses.

Intentionality Makes a Difference

When I started becoming intentional about what I wanted in life and how my business could support me in that process, the change was huge! Instead of feeling like I was a servant to my business, I started seeing my business as the vehicle through which I could make the art I loved, interact with people in a meaningful way and create wealth and freedom for my family. From a practical perspective, that meant I started focusing on my ideal clients instead of trying to make work that pleased everyone. My work schedule considered my clients and normal business hours, but I prioritized my family. In other words, I stopped working 6-7 days a week and began working in the studio 5 days a week, 8am – 4pm. I closed on Sundays. I rarely worked Saturdays because I was able to hire a studio assistant to cover those times for me. The result? More time, more profit, more creativity and yes, more freedom to live life, rather than feeling like an obligated servant to my business.

There was also the fact that I started separating my identity from what did and started focusing on who I am as a person. When you define yourself by your work and what you produce, you'll never measure up! It's a losing proposition because there will always be others who produce more, do more and accomplish more than you do. That's normal. Life is transformed when you realize you are not what you do! I encourage you to give yourself permission to live life beyond what you produce. It will greatly enhance your life and prepare you to accomplish all you've dreamed of.

Now that you see how important profit is to your business and personal wellbeing and that profit fuels business growth, there's a key question you need to ask yourself: *why aren't you pricing for profit now?*

How to Price Your Art

Pricing Barriers

With few exceptions, the number one barrier to pricing for profit is fear. Fear of doing it wrong, fear of not selling your work if you price it too high, even fear of what others might think if you charged market prices. Then there is the general anxiety artists feel when intimidated by the business end of things and not knowing where to start. Trust me, I get it. Been there - felt *all* that.

Limiting Beliefs

In addition to fear, there are also limiting beliefs that paralyze many artists when pricing for profit. These include beliefs like:

- Nobody would pay that for my work
- It's not worth that much… I only have $X in materials
- People in my town (region, country) don't buy expensive art
- My friends say my art is only worth $X
- I would never pay $XXX for my art, so why would anyone else?

The more stock you put in these limiting beliefs, the more they replay in your mind and form superhighways of subconscious belief. These superhighways literally control 99% of your daily activity and can limit or enhance your ability to see and respond to opportunity in your life. I don't have time here to go into a full mindset teaching (You can find that inside my books, *Unlocking the Heart of the Artist* or *Created to Thrive*), but trust me. Whatever you believe about yourself, your work and it's worth, is what you will experience externally. It's a universal law.

The $200 Basket

I can remember it like it was yesterday. I was at my first high-end fine craft show: The Craft Fair of the Southern Highlands. 200+ of the best artists in our region were there and so were our ideal clients. Early on in my career, I had sold my baskets for $25-$50 each. It was a hobby and I never really thought about the pricing. I wasn't trying to grow a business. I simply wanted to make some money on the side and enjoy myself.

Once we moved to Asheville, I started selling my work full-time. I quickly realized my prices had to go up significantly in order to pay the bills and put food on the table at home. So, in preparation for this big show, I increased my prices way beyond what I had ever done before. I even priced one really special piece for $200 (a laughable price today)!

The second day of the show, a man walked up to my booth and was looking at a sculptural piece I created. I could tell he liked it, so I greeted him, and we started chatting. The whole time I'm thinking "Yep, he's going to buy this!" I could just feel it. He talked about how beautiful and unique the piece was as compared to anything else in the show. He complimented me on my craftsmanship. And then, he said "Matt, this is a really special piece." I said thank you, thinking to myself "Yep, he's definitely going to buy this." He continued "And you know people come to this show to find really special pieces. But you know, as much as I like this, $200 just doesn't say 'special'" and he walked away. I couldn't believe it! Needless to say, I was speechless.

That singular experience forced me to confront my own beliefs about my work, it's worth and how to price my art in the marketplace. Thankfully, I learned what I am sharing here with you, and I began to attract my ideal clients and thrive as an artist. My sales steadily increased, and I began selling my work for thousands of dollars with waiting lists for my exclusive commissioned works. Not only did my pricing increase my profit, it exponentially increased my confidence!

The Evil Twins: Compete and Compare

Another limiting mindset is the trap of competition and comparison. This trap causes artists to fear the talent and success of others while degrading their own unique creative voice. At its core, comparison says "I'm not enough. I'll never be as good as them. Why even try?" It's a paralyzing trap that unless overcome, will inhibit an artist from thriving artistically, spiritually and in business.

For most of my life, I struggled with this trap. I saw every talented person I came in contact with as a threat to be conquered rather than a fellow creative to be celebrated. It wasn't until I was able to embrace my own God-given uniqueness and trust the fact that we could both thrive simultaneously that the feeling of competition and comparison left me. As I authentically pursued my art, developed my unique voice, connected with my clients and grew my business without fear or comparison, I realized the sky was the limit!

A big part of knowing who you are uniquely is knowing who you're not! And being ok with that as an artist. As you develop your recognizable artistic voice, attract clients who resonate with your work and build connection with them through your marketing efforts, you will stand out from the crowd! Over time, your confidence will grow along with your business, leaving no place for comparison and no fear of competition.

PART TWO:
The Nitty Gritty of Pricing Your Work

How to Make a Profit on Every Sale

I'm often asked by my students if it's realistic to believe they can make a good profit on every sale, no matter the price point. My answer is always; absolutely! When you know how to price your work with confidence and with profit in mind, it's a no brainer. It just comes down to understanding a simple pricing framework and how pricing works. Once you understand how to input the data, "Shazam!" you'll have profit on every sale.

Pricing for Profit

Now that you understand profit is both important and possible for your art business, I want to share the simple principles I've discovered about pricing so you can use them to transform your business, starting right now.

(I've created a free, easy-to-use PDF to help you in this process. Download it now from the link below)

MattTommeyMentoring.com/artpricingtool

Let's walk through the process of developing a profit-centered pricing strategy that works for you. To make this formula work you have to understand what expenses contribute to the art making and art selling process. Later, I'll show you how profit fits into this equation as we build a pricing framework together.

We'll start by listing the price of materials, then add all other expenses to that. Here is a list to get you started:

Art Materials (your required tools & supplies)
+ **Labor** (what you get paid per hour + employees/contractors)

- **Business Expenses** (heat, air, rent, cell phone, internet, security, etc.)
- <u>**+ Additional Markup** (add at least 20% to all of the above)</u>
- = **Wholesale** (your price to galleries / retail stores)
- x 2 = **Retail** (your price to customers)

Fixed & Variable Costs

In general, there are 2 kinds of costs: fixed costs and variable costs.

Fixed costs for an artist are expenses that are stable and don't change based on the work you are producing. For example, they include expenses like:

- Studio rent
- Utilities
- Phone and internet access
- Marketing and advertising
- Memberships (Collectives, guilds, associations, etc.)

Variable costs are costs that change based on how busy you are or what you're creating. For example, they often include expenses like:

- Cost of Materials & Supplies

- Packing & Shipping
- Printing & Reproduction
- Framing or Presentation
- Labor (Yours and any employees or contractors)
- Commissions or Royalties

Most artists have pretty stable fixed and variable costs unless each project is completely unique. For example, most painters are purchasing the same type of materials at the same rate (canvases, paint, brushes, solvents, etc.); so it becomes easy to project how much it costs, in general, to run your studio each month. Knowing that average number is very helpful when determining your cost formula. However, if you create unique works where material costs vary, you can always calculate your material costs on an individual project basis. Just make sure you double your cost when including it in your final price.

Determining Your Overhead

Overhead is what we generally refer to as the average cost it takes to run your business on a monthly basis. You find this by adding your monthly fixed costs to your monthly variable costs, then taking the average of those numbers over a 3-6 month period. This will give you a solid average overhead from which to operate and project sales, taking into account seasonal fluctuations.

Here's an example of how to calculate your overhead:

Average Fixed Costs: $2030/a month

- Studio rent: $1000
- Utilities: $200
- Phone and internet access: $300
- Marketing and advertising: $500
- Memberships: $30

Average Variable Costs: $4500/a month

- Cost of Materials & Supplies: $500
- Packing & Shipping: $200
- Printing & Reproduction: $300
- Miscellaneous: $300
- Your Labor ($20/hr.): $3200

Now add the fixed and variable totals together: $6,530. This is your monthly average overhead.

How does overhead affect the pricing of your art?

Once you know the average monthly overhead for your studio, you can divide that by week, day or even hour to use that number in your art pricing calculation. This is the cost (by hour, day or week) that it takes to run your studio and create art.

Here's the breakdown using our example from above:

Total Monthly Overhead: $6,530

- Hourly (8-hour day)[1]: $41
- Per Day (5 days per week)[2]: $328
- Per Week (4 weeks per month): $1628

Now, based on the example above, every time you spend a full day creating a piece of art, the bare minimum you would have to charge just to keep the lights on would be $328. But that doesn't take into account your profit or any kind of markup. And how does that overhead pricing translate into specific pieces of art as they vary by size and complexity?

---

[1] Assumes 5 days/week or 20 days/month
[2] Assumes an 8-hour workday

Additional Markup and Retail Pricing

Remember, profit is what gives you the freedom and capacity to grow and thrive. This is where you can experience exponential financial growth because, unless you bring on a lot of staff or have a really expensive studio space, most of your overhead is going to be reasonable. Enter, profit.

Your additional markup is the percentage you're going **to add** to your overhead cost in order to build in some room for unexpected costs and additional income. A great place to start is 20%. As your reputation grows and demand for your work increases, this percentage can grow exponentially. That's when pricing gets to be fun!

Continuing with our calculations:

Monthly Overhead: $6530 + 20% Additional Markup ($1306) = $7836

- Hourly (8-hour day)[3]: $49 x's 8
- Per Day (5 days per week)[4]: $392 x's 5
- Per Week (4 weeks per month): $1960 x's 4 = 7,840 + 20% (1,568) = 9,408

This basic calculation covers your cost <u>with</u> profit **when selling directly to a retail store or to a gallery wholesale or on consignment.** But that's not the end of the pricing story.

What's the Difference between Wholesale and Consignment?

Consignment is when a gallery or store offers to sell your work with no upfront payment to you. The artist is usually paid within 30 days of the sale. While

---

[3] Assumes 5 days/week or 20 days/month
[4] Assumes an 8-hour workday

consignment rates vary based on the gallery, a 50% sales commission is customary.

Wholesale refers to clients who purchase your work outright for resale in their store. This is very common with fine craft artists like jewelers, potters, and fiber artists. Many times these purchases happen at wholesale shows where buyers come to purchase work from multiple artists in one venue. It's also common for wholesale buyers to approach artists at shows, festivals, online or in-studio. Most artists find it helpful to have a minimum purchase requirement (dollar amount or number of pieces) for a wholesale purchase. If you're going to sell wholesale to multiple stores, create a wholesale catalog of your work that clearly states wholesale/retail prices, minimum purchase requirements, production time frames and other terms and conditions.

Sometimes, a gallery or retail store will do a combination purchase from an artist. It's common to purchase smaller items wholesale and then take several larger pieces on consignment. This is beneficial from a cash flow perspective for both the artist and the store owner.

Calculating Your Retail Price

So how do these numbers make their way into your retail pricing? I'm glad you asked. While each artistic medium has its own nuance in pricing, I've found most artists price their work using one of the following starting points:

- Linear inch/cm[5]
- Square inch/cm[6]
- Hourly rate[7]

The reason I say "starting point" is pricing art, even with a formula, is subjective. There are so many variables that affect pricing (we'll discuss those as you continue reading) but a formula gets you in the neighborhood of having a reasonable and consistent

---

[5] Adding the length + width together ie: 36"+48" = 84
[6] Multiplying the length x width together ie: 36" x 48" = 1728
[7] Tracking how many hours a piece takes to create and attributing an hourly rate ie: 8 hours x $20/hr = $160

price. Remember, pricing your art is an art, not a science.

Let's say for example a painter estimates 8 hours of work to create a 36"x48" painting. Minimum, based on our previous calculations, the painter has to generate $392 (8 hours of overhead). Understanding that his painting is comprised of 1728 square inches, it's going to take $4.67/linear inch or $.23/square inch just to cover costs, get paid and make 20% profit. However, that's not the retail price.

In order to get to a retail price (the amount you would sell to the public), you would need to multiply that price times 2. This takes into account the customary 50% markup for most galleries and retailers. This would take the minimum price of this example piece to $784, ensuring the artist covered their overhead and made their minimum profit.

Now, for all you experienced artists out there, I can hear you saying, "but Matt, that's way too low!" Yes, I understand. Most mid-career painters are charging (at the time of this publication) between $2-$6/square inch, with some emerging artists being in the $1/square inch range or less. That would make this example piece somewhere between $1728 - $10,368 retail. What does that mean? It means there's plenty of room to increase your profit margin as the market will bear. We'll talk more about those factors in a moment.

The same pricing methodology can be used with any fine art or fine craft medium you might be using. Some fine craft artists calculate by the hour and others by the square inch or linear foot. There's no hard and fast pricing rule you must follow.

In other words, keep it simple. As long as your overhead is covered with plenty of profit, everything else is additional revenue to help you build your business and thrive as an artist. As you gain experience in the marketplace and understand what the market will bear with regards to the price of your work, you can continue to increase that profit margin percentage to whatever you like.

Additional Considerations When Pricing Your Work

Pass-Through Expenses

I recommend artists consider in their normal pricing all packing, shipping, insurance and sales tax. These are commonly known as pass-through expenses, meaning they are passed through to the client **on top of** their retail price.

For example, if you sold the painting we just talked about for $1728 and it cost $175 to ship and insure, plus 7% sales tax (varies by locality) of $120.96, that's a total of $2,023.96.

Framing and other included presentation items (pedestals, hanging systems, lighting, etc.) must also be included when they are unique to a specific art piece. For example, if a client wants a specific frame or pedestal and you have to order it from another vendor (at wholesale), it's typical to double the price when you sell it to the client. Or if you have these items in stock, you can add that into the original price for the piece, knowing that your costs are covered in the final sale.

Cost of materials and labor

Some artists work with materials that are costly while other artists, like me, work with materials that are mostly inexpensive. If you're having to purchase large amounts of paint, clay, canvases, panels, stones, precious metals, etc., then material cost is something you need to take seriously. Purchasing in bulk and from wholesale suppliers will definitely benefit you in the long run as you build your studio practice.

What materials and supplies could you start purchasing in bulk or from wholesale distributors to get discounts?

In addition, labor can be a significant expense as well, but one well worth it. As I mentioned previously, hiring a studio assistant or other contractors can have an exciting multiplying effect on your production capabilities. However, make sure that you're adequately accounting for all the related expenses associated with their employment as you calculate your pricing. Your licensed CPA or financial professional might be the best at helping you through this process.

Your Competition

I'm not a big proponent of fearing your competition. The way I figure it, God made each of us unique and there's plenty of room for everyone's creative expression. That being said, researching what your competition is charging and how they are marketing their work can be extremely helpful when trying to determine a baseline to begin with. Finding out what's customary within the marketplace can be very beneficial.

As you look across the competitive landscape of other artists with a similar level of expertise doing essentially the same type of work you do, find out the answers to these questions:

- What are they charging per square inch, linear inch or hour?
- What shows are they participating in?
- Do they offer discounts?
- How are they communicating with their clients?
- Where are they selling their work?
- What are they doing on social media, their website and email?

Getting a glimpse into your competitors world, especially their pricing world, can be invaluable as you get started on pricing your work for profit. That's exactly what I did when I started out selling my work professionally. I sat down with several well-known artists both in and out of my specific genre to learn how they developed their pricing models. I researched successful artists in my field and uncovered their pricing, shows, exhibitions and ultimately, business model. Once I knew the lay of the land, so to speak, I then customized an approach that worked for me, taking into consideration my skill, aesthetic, locale and popularity as an artist.

A sage friend and artist mentor offered me excellent advice when I asked about their pricing. "I charge an amount I'd be willing to do it again for. If I wouldn't do it again for the price I originally charged, then I didn't charge enough." A simple but powerful truth.

Create multiple price points in your work

Sometimes people who are not the biggest spenders can be your most passionate fans! Even though they may not bring the most dollars into your world, they are worth considering. I recommend you create 3 price points in your collection: low, medium and high. Examples might include: varying sizes of work, reproductions, enhanced reproductions and originals, production pieces of various sizes and one-of-a-kinds, commissions, and off the shelf work. The possibilities are endless. The more you sell, the more you will discover what resonates with your clientele. Don't be afraid to adjust your prices and product offerings over time. That's a normal business practice.

Reproduction, Prints & Merchandise

Offering reproductions of your work is a great way to sell your work at a lower price point, supplying your best clients with an affordable piece of your art. Remember, word of mouth will increase your sales. It's easy to create multiple sizes on a variety of merchandising products. Depending on many of the factors we've discussed, your reproductions could command a healthy price in the marketplace. A good starting price point for a reproduction the same size as the original is 20-30% of the original's price. For example, if your original piece was $2,500 then a reproduction of the same size might be $500 - $750. Obviously, smaller sizes would be offered at lower prices in a tiered fashion. At the very least, make sure you're asking 3x what it cost you to reproduce your original designs. This goes for any merchandise as well. An example would be; if it costs $100 to create a print (or merchandise), then you would give it a retail price of $300. Remember, you've already made a nice profit when you sold the original piece. The rest is additional income with very little expense.

The best time to increase your price

There's no set formula or timeframe for when you should increase your prices. However, one of the time-honored triggers I always pay attention to is speed and volume of sales. If you're actively selling your art in volume and at a pace you're comfortable with, you can raise your prices 10% each year without anyone noticing. If your work begins to sell faster than you can produce it, a 20% or higher raise might be appropriate.

Bottom line, there are two ways to increase revenue as an artist: make and sell more art or charge more for the art you're making. Over the years, I've done both. I hired a studio assistant and contractors to help me produce the work and harvest the materials I needed to increase production. At the same time, I increased my prices. Together, these strategies significantly increased profits as well as providing me with more time to create and sell.

PART THREE:
Seven Factors that Affect Pricing

Now that you understand how to create a basic pricing strategy for your business, let me introduce you to seven factors that can exponentially increase (or decrease) your art prices. These exponential multipliers include: Quality of the Work, Reputation of the Artist, Word of Mouth, Perception, Client Niche, Where the Work is Sold, and the Availability of the Work.

Quality of the Work and Perception

The Foundational Starting Point

Every artist starts out as a hobbyist; creating what they love because they enjoy the creative process. There are no strings or heavy expectations attached. However, as artists grow and want to turn their attention to selling art in the marketplace among other professional and semi-professional artists, the issue of quality is foundational.

I always tell my students that creating great work is not a mythical destination on their artist journey. It's the foundational starting point on which everything you do as an artist is built. You can have an incredible website, be the best marketer in the world, and have a phenomenal social media following; but at the end of the day, your work speaks. Don't allow yourself to become creatively lazy. Resist the desire to rest on your past creative success. Push through. Dream big. Work hard.

When a client is looking for one-of-a-kind original art, quality is one of the first considerations. It says this artist cares about what they are creating. They are meticulous and detailed oriented. They paid attention to the details because the little things matter.

When I create a piece of work, I push myself to make it with longevity in mind. I call it the Antiques Roadshow test. You know; the TV show on PBS where people bring their antiques hoping to cash in on some lost treasure that's been hanging around in the attic. I want my work to stand the test of time. And who knows, someday an art curator might say about my work; "My goodness, it's a little dusty but it is still a masterpiece." Quality speaks and people are willing to pay for it.

People's perception creates their reality regardless of how true that perception may be. And, perception has a huge impact, not only on what you can charge for your work but also what they are willing to pay.

That's not an invitation to create a false narrative with empty promises. No! Rather, it's a call to understand the importance of how your clients, potential clients, fans, followers and referral partners perceive you (and your art). Their positive perception of you and your work is crucial to your success as an artist.

One of the ways I've enhanced the perception of my work over the years is by developing a concierge approach to creating art for my clients. After a consultation in their home, I would harvest materials from their mountain property and create a one-of-a kind special piece just for them. Because of that relationship and level of trust, I'm often invited to install the pieces myself. These are breathtaking 2 to

10 million-dollar homes made even more beautiful when my art is installed!

Having the ability to photograph my work in these spaces, with my client's permission of course, immediately creates the perception online and in magazines that my work is high-end, unique and worthy of a high price.

As much as you can, enhance the perception of your worth through association with organizations, people and opportunities that are esteemed by your ideal clients. Doing so will have a positive effect on your pricing and ultimately your sales.

How do your current clients and prospects perceive you and the work you create?

When you consider the quality of your own artwork, what are some areas of improvement you can make? How can you communicate the quality of your work to your potential clients?

Reputation

Benjamin Franklin wisely said, "*It takes many good deeds to build a reputation, and only one bad one to lose it.*" True words. Your reputation as an artist and business person precedes you. Whether it be at a show, exhibition, business meeting with a new gallery or online; someone is checking your Google reviews. Your reputation can either be a highway to opportunity or an immediate roadblock.

If someone were to ask your ten most recent clients about you, what would they say? How about gallery owners or referral partners who've worked with you over the years? What can you do to ensure you have a stellar reputation among clients, peers and partners?

I remember a very talented blacksmith who about lost his business. People were calling and he wouldn't call them back. He was defaulting on jobs after already taking a deposit. He had to basically start over because of the damage to his reputation. Not an easy journey.

I've also seen the opposite. I've had people commission my work for thousands of dollars simply on the value of my reputation and a referral. The beautiful thing? Price wasn't at the top of their questions. Why? They trusted me and expected my work to be excellent based on what they'd heard. The better your reputation, the higher the trust factor in you as an artist.

Word of Mouth

Over the years word of mouth advertising has steadily moved my price upwards. Why? Because one word from a client who loves you and your work is worth a lot more than any advertising campaign you could ever employ.

One day I received a call from my friend Carol, an interior designer I had collaborated with before. She wanted to know if I would be willing to speak to her garden club. Though I honestly wondered what in the world I would talk about, to honor the relationship, I agreed. I prepared a 45-minute talk, loaded up my work and took off for the meeting. When I arrived, I was warmly greeted by the attendees. 50 wealthy ladies, clients and friends of Carol's, were gathered there. Ladies that loved art and all things southern.

As I set up my work some wandered over to say they had heard wonderful things about me. When it was time, my well-respected friend rose to introduce me: *"Ladies, I've known Matt for several years and I just love his work. In fact, last year, after I designed the outdoor porch for the Designer Show House, I needed some special pieces to complete the room. And ladies, I've learned when you need something special, you call Matt Tommey."*

Well, you could have knocked me over with a feather! I gave my talk, took a few questions and then opened for sales. The ladies rushed the table. One sale came after another. I remember throwing checks on the floor behind my table just to keep up. I sold almost my entire inventory in less than 30 minutes.

Not only was that a great singular event, it led to numerous - and I mean numerous - other invitations to attend and speak at other garden clubs around the southeastern United States. I never spent a dime in advertising. Better still, because of the reputation (and referral) of those inviting me, my prices continually increased.

Referral Protocol

Working with strategic referral partners over the years like the one I mentioned in the previous story has been one of my most successful strategies in my art business. Learning to develop and nurture those relationships is foundational for all artists. Doing so ensures a constant stream of business even with seasonal or economic conditions change. For example, during shutdowns caused by the COVID-19 Pandemic, I was still receiving commission inquiries from my strategic partners. Since the luxury real estate market was booming at the time, their clients were building, remodeling and purchasing original art!

Many of my mentoring students ask me if referral partners expect a discount or referral fee when referring my work? The answer to this question depends on the relationship. In general, if you're working with a designer or firm who is seeking your work for resale with no prior relationship, they will probably expect a discount of 20-30%. Many designers that work with artists simply refer their clients to the artist directly and don't expect a referral fee. That's largely been my experience. Some of my best clients have been designers, builders and furniture store owners who enjoyed introducing me to their clients. No financial remuneration was ever expected or requested. However, I always go out of my way to make sure they know I am thankful for the referral. A bouquet of their favorite flowers or providing lunch for their office goes a long way!

Ways to Enhance the Perception of Your Work

Take a moment and brainstorm some ideas regarding how you can enhance the perception your clients and prospects have about you. Consider these questions:

- Is your website a high-end representation of you and your work?
- What makes you stand out from the crowd as unique and special, rather than the typical artist in the market?
- What about awards, accolades, editorials or recognitions you could bring to the forefront of your marketing?

- Do you have images of your artwork in high-end locations like homes or commercial spaces?
- Are you using testimonials from satisfied clients and partners to enhance your brand story?

Learning to tell your brand story in a way that makes you stand out from the crowd is essential when pricing and selling your work for top dollar. Speak directly to your customer in a way that empathizes with their desires. Make them feel special by speaking about things that are important to them. When people like you, what you create and the way you do business, they will refer and purchase from you. That likeability factor creates a bond of trust that's invaluable in the marketplace.

Your Personal Brand

You have seconds to connect with a potential client online. The more clear and detailed information you can give them about your work helps them make an informed buying decision. List the attributes that make you stand out from the other artists who essentially do the same thing you do. Amplify and repeat these characteristics in ways that connect with the desires of your ideal client and you'll be well on your way to curating a powerful personal brand!

Discounts and Bonuses

I'm not a big fan of discounts, especially for new clients. I think it trains them to look for future buying incentives rather than focusing on their connection to your work. That being said, you can use discounts effectively when working with clients who are purchasing multiple works at once or as a returning client reward. I would encourage you to use discounts to incentivize the actions *you* want, not as bait for new customers.

Consider adding bonuses before employing a discount strategy. A well-designed bonus can enhance the customer experience and build deeper relationships in ways discounts can never accomplish. For example, I created a book of my work called, "Every Basket Begins with a Walk in the Woods".

This book includes retrospective images of my work and journey as an artist along with poetic reflections written by me. It cost me $6 to produce through KDP Amazon and I sell autographed copies on my website for $30. As a bonus for my clients, I like to include an autographed copy with their purchase. It's a nice way to say thank you and enhances their experience.

What about Discounts for Friends and Family?

I want to suggest you do not offer discounts to friends and family. Here is why; As an artist who is also an entrepreneur, art is how you produce your income. This is your business. And as I always say, *"You can't have business dreams with hobby habits."* When you give discounts, you're giving away your profit. And profit is how you grow and thrive in business. But let me also dig a little deeper. Usually, this question comes to me from artists who feel pressured to give discounts to friends and family. That's never a good situation for any of us.

In this scenario, I recommend you politely let them know that this is your business and that you're already pricing your work in a manner that reflects normal pricing for artwork of similar caliber. You should never give a discount because you feel pressured. However, if you want to give a piece as a gift, under no compulsion to do so, then that's completely up to you! I've done that many times and there's great joy in giving your art as a gift. Just don't feel pressured to do so. When someone isn't willing to pay full price for your work, it's their issue, not yours.

When you give away your work, you're also degrading the perception of your work. This especially comes into play when you consider donating your work to non-profit auctions and the like. While where are times when this can be appropriate, most of the time your work ends up being purchased for much less than market value. If you have a non-profit you want to support, great! Sell your work and give the money you want to give.

Scarcity and Leverage

I believe serious artists should have a good inventory of work available at all times yet there's a surprising factor I want to teach you about called "scarcity". It's a concept that I recognized was at work early on in my business. Once I understood how it worked, I intentionally began using it to increase the desirability of my art in the marketplace.

If there's less of something, people want it more. This is scarcity. And it can increase the perceived value of your art. You know how it is; you want the dessert you can't have, stand in line all night for concert tickets that are sure to sell out in seconds. We've all fallen prey to it because it's just a part of the human condition. It's how most people see and respond to life's opportunities.

I employed the scarcity technique in my art business through focusing on the creation of commissioned works. Although you could walk into my gallery and studio at any time to purchase a smaller piece or see examples of my work, I never had my large wall sculptures available for sale. I positioned them as unique works created for specific clients and spaces in mind. This created a mystique around my work that made my ideal clients desire it even more. The underlying thought was "Not everyone has this… it's unique, it's special, it's limited."

When I first started doing this, I could create commissioned works within a week or two with no problem. I was just happy to have the work! However, as my art business grew, the timeline for my commissioned work had to be extended. At first it was a couple of weeks, then a couple of months, then 6 months before I could deliver a piece. But here's the crazy thing: the longer it took, the more people wanted it and the more they were willing to pay. Why? Because subconsciously "scarcity" added perceived value to my work. As you're creating the price points and collections of work for your business, don't be afraid to offer commissions with longer delivery cycles. It just might be the revenue booster you never knew you had!

Are you currently employing any scarcity strategies in your art business? If not, how could you begin to create the perception of limited availability to enhance how others perceive your work?

Leverage

Lastly, a phenomenon I call leverage allows you to create momentum in your business without creating additional work for yourself. Leverage is employing strategies that allow you to exponentially multiply your results without multiplying your efforts. In other words, work smarter, not harder. It can include things like selling online versus always traveling for in-person shows. Starting a referral program for existing clients. Developing strategic partnerships with non-competing professionals already doing business with your ideal clients. Even hiring contract, part-time or full-time studio assistants to create work, prepare for upcoming projects, handle administrative tasks or manage your social media, website, or even, gallery. Strategies like these allow you to focus on what you really want to be doing: making art.

One example of leverage I used was the hiring of contract labor to harvest my raw materials for me. Although I loved getting out in the forest to harvest my own materials for making woven sculpture, having a retail gallery in a busy arts district severely limited my ability to get out in the woods. As with any business, I had to examine the tasks that needed to be done and determine whether or not they had to be done exclusively by me. If not, then it's an opportunity for leverage. In other words, if I could hire and train someone to do the same task at the same level of quality for significantly less than I would pay myself, it's a win.

Instead of spending weeks of my year harvesting truckloads of raw materials for my basketry – vines, bark, driftwood – I hired and trained contractors to do that work for me. They were responsible for locating, harvesting and delivering these materials to me based on my specifications. The result? More time in the studio for making and client interaction, something I alone could do. Even better, I had a constant supply of materials ready at all times. Then, if I wanted to head out to the woods for inspiration or to find a special piece for a project, I could. There was no pressure of having to harvest in volume. Problem solved. Solution: leverage.

This practice of employing contract labor and also studio assistants is very common in working artist studios. From jewelers to potters, sculptors to painters, there are jobs that need to be done but don't have to be done by you. Find the right people. Train them well and you'll create more time, profit and creative brain space for yourself.

Frugality or Fear?

So many artists employ strategies around saving money and reducing costs rather than having an investment perspective. Saving money and reducing costs are a temporary (and sometimes needed) short-term solution that will never position you for growth. Moreover, frugality becomes fear when your belief in "not enough" becomes greater than the promise of "more than enough". While there's nothing inherently wrong with frugality (I love to save money and get a good deal) there's only so much scrimping and saving you can do. And that's never going to grow your art business. A poverty mentality only focuses on reducing expenses and doing enough to make ends meet.

Investing in your business might seem foreign to you and that's ok. Like most artists, you're probably pretty good at just about everything you pursue. Because of that, it seems easier to just do everything yourself without the hassle of involving others. Trust me, I had the same thoughts and lived with the frustration of limited growth. But here's the truth: the more you cultivate this mindset, the more you will become the bottleneck to your own success. There's only so much you can do.

An abundance mentality focuses on creating and attracting solutions that will produce growth. It embraces investment in your business, realizing that growth only comes with intentionality. Abundance sees your business as a garden to be tended, rather than an out-of-control list of expenses to be tamed.

How can you begin to create leverage in your own business to increase profits, reduce stress and work in your areas of strength?

Create a Client Niche

Like most artists, I started out thinking everyone was my client. I was sorely mistaken. Not everyone who walks through the door of your studio is going to be your ideal customer. Trust me. I found that out the hard way! If you take a shotgun approach in selling your art, it rarely produces the results you're looking for. But if you learn to listen and pay attention to your clients, they will provide you with mountains of intel that will inform your sales process, pricing, marketing and even guide your artistry.

I learned the primary clients for my locally sourced woven sculptures were right here, in the mountains of Western North Carolina. Wealthy professionals living in luxury vacation or retirement homes with a high expectation of service, quality and attention to detail. Clients that value unique artistry and wanted something different than what their friends or neighbors had. For these clients, price is not the driving motivation and the sky's the limit.

Once I discovered my niche, I focused on how to create intersections with them at events they frequented and looked for opportunities to connect. I became known, respected and referred to within these communities. Ultimately, because of this niche, I never had to look for work again.

As you cultivate a stellar reputation for quality and service, you too will develop a niche of clients; a group of similar people who relate to you and your work. The quicker you identify your niche clients and develop a referral network made up of clients who like and trust you, the quicker you'll begin to see your art business flourish. Again, having the right people on your side and excited about your work is absolutely invaluable.

Location, Location, Location

Because perception is so crucial in pricing, marketing, and selling your art; the locations where you sell your work is vital. It can literally be the difference between causing confusion and making a sale.

When you're starting out; you need to get your work in front of as many people as possible just to gather data. What sells, what's connecting, who's interested? As you collect this intel, use it to identify and pursue your ideal client. Create intersection points where your paths will cross, and relationships will develop.

Your Ideal Client

The questions below will provide you a window into your ideal clients' world:

- Where do they shop?
- What do they do for fun?
- What non-profit organizations do they support?

- What trusted advisors do they consult in their buying decisions?
- How important is the reputation of the gallery that carries your work?
- Do they consider 'where' your work is being shown a statement of value?

Though many people struggle to verbalize their internal motivations for buying art, they are definitely having an internal conversation. Where you show your work and the venues you choose to sell through have a big impact on how people perceive you and your art and ultimately, it's value. At the end of the day, 100% of those perceptions are reflected in what they are willing to pay for your work.

One weekend I was showing my work at a community street fair and art show in Asheville as I'd done many times before. This time I was placed between a multi-level marketing cosmetics distributor and someone selling artificial floral arrangements and wreaths. Since my prices were on the rise and not congruent with the audience in attendance, my sales that day were low. During the course of the day, I heard one of my newer clients call out my name in surprise. They had recently purchased a piece of my work at a higher end show and hadn't expected to see me at this souped-up street festival. It was awkward, and I imagined them thinking "Hey, I thought you were really somebody…" Their perception of me and where I was selling my work that day were not in agreement. Because of the relationship I was building with them, they did buy another piece that day, but suffice it to say, I learned something that propelled me forward. I never sold my work at that show again. Not because it was a bad show; but because my reputation, client niche and perception had moved beyond it.

Another time I participated in a small community craft fair in the town where most of my ideal clients have vacation homes. I thought it was the perfect place to intersect with my niche clients but I quickly learned they didn't want to purchase original art at an outdoor craft fair. Why? Perception. I had the right people, but the wrong venue. Later that summer I was a guest artist at a highly regarded furniture and interior design store in the same area. I sold out and received months of work, all from that Saturday afternoon opportunity. Why? Perception. I had the right people in the right place, endorsed by people they respected. The end result? Increased sales.

Frequently Asked Questions

Now that you understand the basics of how to create a consistent pricing model and many of the variables that affect pricing, I want to answer some of the common questions I get from artists.

Where do I start if I've never sold my work?

If you're brand new to selling your art (or just coming back into the market) I recommend a few things. Research the market to see what artists in your medium and at your career status level are charging; both regionally and nationally. This will give you a good ballpark for what the market will bear. Then, using the pricing formula I've provided for you in this book, create a consistent pricing strategy that works for you. Optimally, you want to be in the middle of the market, not too expensive or too cheap. Remember; perception drives sales. If you price your work too low, potential clients may feel it's not worth investing in, resulting in fewer sales.

Lastly, test and measure. You have to start somewhere. Choose a pricing structure you feel good about, get out into the marketplace and see what happens. You may be pleasantly surprised and need to increase your prices sooner than you think.

Should I charge more for my commissions?

Hopefully after reading this book you understand the importance of creating a consistent pricing model for your business. Assuming that's the case, I'll answer this question by encouraging you to make sure you take into account everything needed to successfully complete a commissioned work for a client. Give yourself some wiggle room for the unknown factors that may arise during the project.

That way, you're sure to cover your costs and make a healthy profit. The better you feel about the experience, the more confidently you'll price commissioned works in the future.

Should I list my prices on my website and social media?

Absolutely. You have seconds to connect with a potential client online. The more clear and detailed information you can give them about your work helps them make an informed buying decision. Be sure to price your items the same on all of your platforms; your website and all social media as well as pieces you have in galleries, shows and other retail environments. You want to honor all partners with consistent pricing.

Should I keep my prices the same in every venue?

Absolutely! This is what I call pricing integrity and it's especially important when you're selling directly to your clients in addition to wholesale or consignment channels. Offering lower prices to clients purchasing directly from you undermines the important relationship you have with galleries and stores who carry your work. Price your work according to the principles I've taught here. Keep your prices the same no matter where you're selling. It takes the drama out of feeling pressured to give discounts and lets your customers (and your selling partners) know you are operating in integrity.

How should I price my art classes?

Although this is a book about pricing your art, teaching classes is a great strategy for most artists as they grow their art business. Just like with your art, the same general rules apply. Make sure your fixed and variable expenses are covered, add in your labor, materials and some room for cushion and profit. Will you provide drinks, snacks or lunch? Just make sure you have all your bases covered. Additionally, research art classes in your local area to make sure you're within the normal range of what others at your experience level are charging. That gives you a starting point to jump into the market and start selling. The more unique your workshops are and the more desirable your classes become, the more you can charge. And who knows! Some of your students may even purchase some of your art while in your classes.

Final Thoughts

What a journey! I'm so honored you allowed me to speak into your sacred journey as an artist. You now have the tools to price your art with confidence. This is a game changer for every artist. The difference between you doing what you love for a living, instead of having to find income from other sources while doing your art on the side. When combined with a solid multi-stream marketing strategy, a healthy mindset and unique desirable artwork, you are sure to have success. I pray that becomes your story. Please let me know of your successes so we can celebrate together!

I've created many additional resources for artists who want to thrive artistically, spiritually and grow their business. To access my blog, podcasts, inspirational devotionals, other books, topical mini courses and learn more about my mentoring program; visit

www.MattTommeyMentoring.com.

For Further Reading

These books have inspired my journey and I encourage you to check them out.

- *The eMyth* by Michael Gerber
- *Influence: The Psychology of Persuasion* by Robert Cialdini
- *The Go-Giver* by Bob Burg
- *Real Artists Don't Starve* by Jeff Goins
- *Purple Cow* by Seth Godin
- *This is Marketing* by Seth Godin
- *Raving Fans* by Ken Blanchard & Sheldon Bowes
- *The War of Art* by Steven Pressfield

About the Author

Matt is a woven sculpture artist from Asheville, North Carolina, and an internationally known Christian speaker, author of several books. He is also a mentor to artists from around the world through his "Created to Thrive" Artist Mentoring Program and The Thriving Christian Artist podcast.

In 2009, God called Matt to "raise up an army of artists to reveal His glory all over the earth." Since then, Matt has given his life to helping artists thrive spiritually, creatively, and in business through creating live events, resources, and online opportunities that equip artists to live the life they were divinely designed to live in the Kingdom.

As an artist, Matt's work has been featured in many magazines, shows, and exhibitions and is mostly commissioned by private clients for luxury mountain and coastal homes around the country. In 2011, Matt was recognized by the Smithsonian American Art Museum's Renwick Gallery as an American Artist Under 40. In 2018, Matt was recognized as one of the Best Artist Mentors in the country by Professional Artist Magazine.

Other Resources from Matt Tommey

Books by Matt Tommey
To see Matt's full line of books, visit
MattTommeyMentoring.com/resources

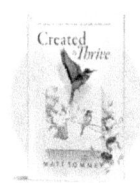

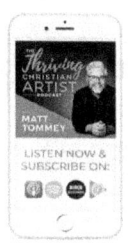

The Thriving Christian Artist Podcast
Matt's podcast can be found at
MattTommeyMentoring.com/podcast

Matt's Blog
If you love the podcast,
then check out Matt's weekly blog that
picks up where the podcast ends found at
MattTommeyMentoring.com/blog

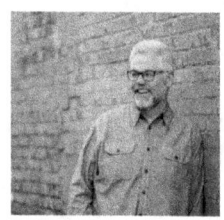

The Artist Mentoring Program

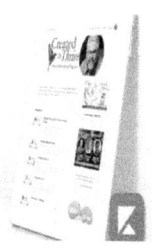

An easy to follow online program dedicated to helping Christian artists become confident and equipped in their creative callings. Learn More, visit
MattTommeyMentoring.com/artmentor

www.ingramcontent.com/pod-product-compliance
Lightning Source LLC
Chambersburg PA
CBHW070427220526
45466CB00004B/1568